Belgian Malinois

Katie Gillespie

AV2

www.openlightbox.com

Step 1
Go to **www.openlightbox.com**

Step 2
Enter this unique code
SXPJOOLHE

Step 3
Explore your interactive eBook!

AV2 is optimized for use on any device

Your interactive eBook comes with...

Contents
Browse a live contents page to easily navigate through resources

Audio
Listen to sections of the book read aloud

Videos
Watch informative video clips

Weblinks
Gain additional information for research

Slideshows
View images and captions

Try This!
Complete activities and hands-on experiments

Key Words
Study vocabulary, and complete a matching word activity

Quizzes
Test your knowledge

Share
Share titles within your Learning Management System (LMS) or Library Circulation System

Citation
Create bibliographical references following the Chicago Manual of Style

This title is part of our AV2 digital subscription

1-Year K–5 Subscription
ISBN 978-1-7911-3320-7

Access hundreds of AV2 titles with our digital subscription.
Sign up for a FREE trial at **www.openlightbox.com/trial**

All About Dogs

Belgian Malinois

Contents

Name That Dog

Which dog often works with the police and the military?

Which dog loves to be around people?

Which dog is called a "Mal" for short?

Which dog needs plenty of exercise?

Did you guess the Belgian Malinois?

You are right!

Belgian Malinois History

As their name suggests, Belgian Malinois are from Belgium. They were first bred near the city of Malines, which is where the term Malinois comes from. These dogs are often simply called "Mals."

The first Mals came to the United States in 1911. The **breed** did well in the country for many years. However, Malinois numbers started to drop during the **Great Depression**. During **World War II**, fewer Mals were available for breeding because they could not be brought from Europe to the United States.

Belgium is a country in Europe. It is bordered by the Netherlands, Germany, Luxembourg, and France, as well as the North Sea.
North Sea
Netherlands
Germany
Belgium
Luxembourg
France

In 1959, the Belgian Malinois was recognized by the American Kennel Club (AKC). This organization classifies dog breeds into seven different categories. These groupings are determined by a breed's function and heritage. Dogs in each category share certain common traits.

Mals belong to the AKC's Herding Group. Breeds in this category are able to help people control the movement of animals such as cows, sheep, or goats. Other members of the herding group include border collies, German shepherds, and Australian cattle dogs.

By the early 1960s, the U.S. Belgian Malinois population had started to go up again, thanks to increased breeding by fans of the breed. In recent years, Mals have quickly become more popular than ever before. They were ranked at number 37 on the AKC's 2020 list of most popular dog breeds. This was a jump of more than 20 spots in less than a decade.

In some countries, Mals are grouped with three other types of Belgian herding dogs as a single breed. Known as Belgian shepherd dogs, this group also includes the Laekenois, Tervuren, and Groenendael breeds.

Mals are often confused with German shepherds. However, a Belgian Malinois has a shorter coat and is more lightly built than a German shepherd.

What Mals Look Like

Mals are medium to large dogs. Females stand about 22 to 24 inches (56 to 61 centimeters) high. They weigh between 40 and 60 pounds (18 and 27 kilograms). Males are larger than females. They are 24 to 26 inches (61 to 66 cm) high and weigh 60 to 80 pounds (27 to 36 kg).

A Mal's **coat** is short and straight, with a dense undercoat. The coat comes in many colors, ranging from **fawn** to mahogany, with black tips on each hair. The fur on a Mal's ears, head, and lower legs is quite short. It is longer on the tail, on the backs of the thighs, and around the neck.

Rather than walking in a straight line, Mals tend to move in a large circle.

Some Mals have white toe tips with matching white nails.

These elegant dogs are known for the way in which they proudly hold up their heads. They have a flat forehead and a black pattern called a mask on their face. Their nose and lips are also black, along with their small, triangular ears. Mals have brown to dark brown eyes, which are slightly almond-shaped.

Mals have a square-shaped, well-balanced body. They have a firm back and a curved tail. Although they are solid, Mals are not bulky. Their legs are strong and muscular. This allows them to move freely and easily, with a smooth, fast **gait**.

A Mal's feet are similar in appearance to those of a cat. They are well padded, with toes that curve close together. Most Mals have strong black nails.

A Mal may be born with floppy ears. They will stiffen and stand up by the time the dog is about four months old.

A Loyal Companion

Mals are confident and alert. They are known for being extremely intelligent. Mals are also very hardworking animals. These qualities are what make them such effective herding dogs.

Although they have many positive traits, Mals are not the right fit for every owner. They tend to be highly energetic and sensitive animals. This is why they are not typically recommended for first-time dog owners.

Mals enjoy accompanying their owners on long hikes or bike trips.

Mals want to be near their family at all times. They should not be left alone for long periods of time.

Mals require plenty of exercise. This means that their owners must be active as well. Since they are such athletic dogs, Mals are not very well suited to living in apartments or other small spaces. They need plenty of room to train and play.

Mals love to be around people. For the right owners, they make great companions. Since Mals often form close bonds, owners must be willing to give them all the attention they need. In return, these dogs will be loyal and responsive to directions.

Mals are affectionate with their families, but may try to herd them, too. They are usually good with children, especially if brought up together, but should be supervised around them. Mals may act reserved or indifferent toward strangers until they get to know them.

Mal Puppies

A breed's size affects the number of puppies in a **litter**. Generally, large dogs have more puppies than small dogs. Mals usually have litters of about 6 to 10 puppies.

Unless they are raised alongside them, and properly trained, some Mals can be **aggressive** toward other pets. As with all dogs, Mal puppies need **socialization** in order to prevent this. Once they are old enough, Mal puppies should meet a variety of dogs, people, and other animals. This will help them grow into well-socialized adults.

Mals are known for having a high "play drive." They often consider tasks they are given to be games.

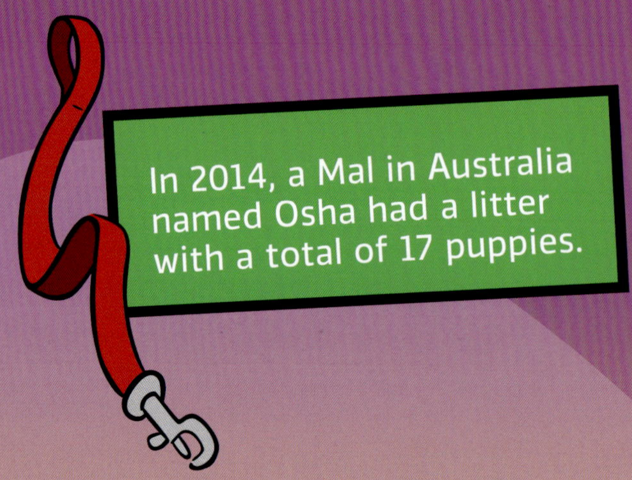

Obedience classes are a good opportunity for Mal puppies to have new experiences. They will also learn important skills. Mals are eager to please. This makes them fairly easy to train.

Mal puppies need physical activity from a young age. Exercise should start slowly and increase gradually over time. For younger puppies, daily play should be enough. Short walks can be added to a puppy's daily routine as it grows. A puppy's playtime can be also increased as the dog grows. Since their joints and bones are still developing, Mals should avoid hard surfaces on walks. The dogs can walk farther and for longer as they mature.

By one year of age, Mals are at 90 percent of their adult weight. However, most do not reach their full adult weight for another year.

During World War I, Belgian Malinois dogs helped carry messages and find wounded soldiers.

Natural Protectors

Mals have always been bred as working dogs. They have a long history of working on farms. Traditionally, their main duties included gathering, herding, and protecting livestock. They were also responsible for watching over the property and the family who lived there.

Today, Mals are still excellent herding dogs. However, this is not their only job. Due to their protective nature, Mals are commonly used for other kinds of work, too.

For instance, Mals are in high demand as police dogs. In addition to being natural guardians, Mals are driven and vigilant. These qualities make them ideal for police work. They often serve as watchdogs as well.

In the United States, Mals have been used by the Secret Service to help guard the White House.

A Mal's outer coat is water resistant. Many of these dogs enjoy swimming and playing in water.

Caring for a Mal

As a breed with a naturally short coat, Mals do not require much grooming. Occasional brushing is enough to remove loose fur for most of the year.

Mals are generally easy to care for, but they do **shed** seasonally. This happens twice a year. During these times, daily brushing will keep them clean and looking their best. Along with grooming, a Mal's nails need to be kept trim and its teeth should be brushed often.

Mals usually reach their adult height when they are about 10 to 11 months old. Some keep growing until they are 18 or 19 months old.

Although Mals do not need a special diet, their food should be approved by a **veterinarian**. Owners should check their dog's weight regularly to make sure it is healthy.

Overall, Mals are a healthy breed. However, like other dogs, they can have certain health conditions. Breeders should test Mals for hip and elbow dysplasia. The dogs should be screened for eye problems as well.

Having a dog is a big responsibility, but it can also be very rewarding. Owners must be prepared to make a lifelong commitment to any pet. This is particularly important if adopting a Mal. They have a long life expectancy of 14 to 16 years.

Although treats can be used for training, too many can cause a Mal to become overweight.

Belgian Malinois Quiz

Q: Why are Mals such effective herding dogs?

A: Because they are confident, alert, extremely intelligent, and very hardworking

Q: How much do female Mals weigh?

A: Between 40 and 60 pounds (18 and 27 kg)

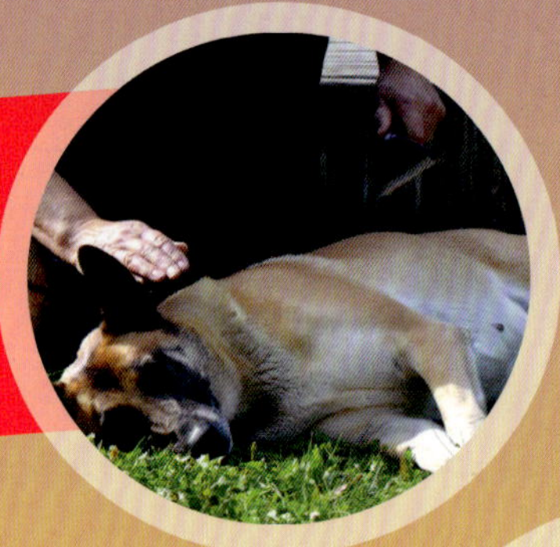

Q: How often should Mals be brushed during shedding season?

A: Daily

Q: Near which Belgian city were Mals first bred?

A: Malines

Q: What color are the nails of most Mals?

A: Black

Q: How many puppies are in a typical Mal litter?

A: 6 to 10

Key Words

aggressive (uh-GREH-suhv): mean or unfriendly; likely to start a fight

breed (BREED): a certain type of an animal

coat (KOHT): a dog's fur

fawn (FAWN): a light yellowish brown color

gait (GAYT): manner of walking

Great Depression (GRAYT duh-PREH-shn): a period of economic trouble that began in 1929

litter (LI-tr): a group of babies born to one animal at the same time

shed (SHED): when fur naturally falls off

socialization (so-shuh-lai-ZAY-shn): helping puppies become comfortable around people and other animals in different environments

veterinarian (veh-truh-NEH-ree-uhn): a doctor who takes care of animals

World War II (WURLD WOR TOO): a war that lasted from 1939 to 1945 and involved many countries around the world

Index

Get the best of both worlds.

AV2 bridges the gap between print and digital.

The expandable resources toolbar enables quick access to content including **videos**, **audio**, **activities**, **weblinks**, **slideshows**, **quizzes**, and **key words**.

Animated videos make static images come alive.

Resource icons on each page help readers to further **explore key concepts**.

Published by Lightbox Learning Inc.
276 5th Avenue, Suite 704 #917
New York, NY 10001
Website: www.openlightbox.com

Library of Congress Control Number: 2022933073

ISBN 978-1-7911-4807-2 (hardcover)
ISBN 978-1-7911-4808-9 (softcover)
ISBN 978-1-7911-4330-5 (multi-user eBook)

Printed in Guangzhou, China
1 2 3 4 5 6 7 8 9 0 26 25 24 23 22

022022
101321

Project Coordinator: John Willis
Designer: Terry Paulhus

Photo Credits
Every reasonable effort has been made to trace ownership and to obtain permission to reprint copyright material. The publisher would be pleased to have any errors or omissions brought to its attention so that they may be corrected in subsequent printings. The publisher acknowledges Alamy, Minden Pictures, Newscom, Getty Images, and Shutterstock as its primary image suppliers for this title.